Table of Contents

Knowledge is power, but the ability to turn knowledge into action is where true success lies

Preface

Life is made up of moments and dreams, each connecting to the next. Along the way, we encounter stories that shape who we become. For me, today marks the fulfillment of a long-held dream—to write a book. They say the stars must align for certain events to unfold, and I couldn't agree more. My journey toward this endeavor has been fuelled by two profound passions: a love for writing and a heartfelt desire to guide students and professionals toward the right career paths.

The spark to write a book first ignited during the formative years of my career. The more books I read, the more my admiration for their authors grew, and with it, my longing to contribute my voice to this vast repository of knowledge. Over time, my work brought me closer to students and job seekers through hiring, training, or mentoring new joiners in the corporate world and through workshops and seminars that I have been passionately conducting through these years. These interactions deepened my understanding of their challenges and strengthened my resolve to create something that could make a real difference.

One insight emerged clearly that many students lack timely and accurate guidance from industry mentors. Without proper direction, students often end up in the wrong jobs or take temporary jobs out of necessity or convenience, only to realize, years later, that these roles were never their true calling. By then, the chance to build their careers on the right path has slipped away, leaving them with lingering regrets and countless "what ifs."

The book aims to bridge this gap. It is designed for students, professionals, and job seekers looking to break into corporate careers. It focuses on **what truly matters today**, offering actionable advice, insider insights, and a roadmap to help readers make informed decisions that align with their career aspirations.

Through this book, my aim is not just to share my experiences but to empower seekers to discover their potential, bypass common career missteps, and walk boldly into the dynamic world of market research. This book is more than a personal milestone for me; it's a heartfelt effort to mentor, inspire, and support those who need it most as they take their baby steps into a meaningful career. If you've ever felt lost or unsure about how to break into market research, this book is for you. If you've ever wondered what skills and strategies matter in today's job market, this book is for you. And if you've ever wished for a mentor to guide you, consider this book your starting point.

Here's to the new beginnings, turning dreams into reality, and making a significant impact in the world of market research. Let's embark on this journey together!

Book Overview

Practical Market Research as the name suggests is your ultimate guide to understanding why market research is indispensable in today's fast-paced economy. Whether you're a student, job seeker, or aspiring professional, this book offers valuable insights, practical tips, and actionable strategies to help you navigate and thrive in this booming field. From understanding the ever-evolving consumer landscape to exploring diverse career paths, this book reveals how market research combines flexibility, creativity, and inclusivity to offer something for everyone.

Packed with real-life case studies, actionable tips, and a deep dive into the skills you need to succeed, this book makes market research approachable and fun. You'll uncover the art of trend-spotting, learn how to build a standout online presence, and get insider tips on turning internships into stepping stones for career growth. More than just a career guide, this book helps you think big, act sharp, and embrace the exciting challenges of a market research career with confidence. So, if you're ready to master the tools of the trade, and set yourself up for success, this book is your launchpad to an extraordinary professional adventure.

About the Author

Mr. Sumant Ugalmugale is a recognized expert in the field of market research and consulting. With over a decade of experience, he has led impactful initiatives in market research and healthcare consulting. He has worked with leading organizations such as IQVIA, Novartis, Global Market Insights, and Trinity Partners, making a notable impact in the field of market research and healthcare consulting. A graduate of Bombay College of Pharmacy, Mumbai, and an MBA in Pharmaceutical Management from the prestigious NIPER, Mohali, his journey exemplifies dedication and excellence. He is passionate about delivering actionable insights that guide informed decisions and help shape the future of the industry.

Beyond his professional expertise, he has a true passion for teaching and mentoring. With a thoughtful and approachable style, he excels at making complex concepts easy to understand and engaging for his students. Through seminars, workshops, and courses at various institutions, he has inspired countless aspiring professionals, helping them navigate their careers with confidence and clarity. His influence extends beyond the classroom, leaving a lasting imprint on the careers of many who have had the privilege of learning from him.

When he's not delivering insightful talks or guiding others in mastering market research, you'll likely find him in a tranquil setting, brainstorming innovative ideas, or simply recharging his creative energy. A true nature enthusiast, he believes that the best ideas emerge in the peaceful solitude of nature.

This book is a reflection of Sumant's journey—both his professional experiences and his philosophy. Infused with his passion for market research, teaching, and empowering others, it is designed to provide practical insights and guidance for those looking to excel in the field. Whether you're a student, a professional, or someone looking to explore the world of market research, Sumant's book is a valuable resource for anyone eager to learn from a true industry leader.

Acknowledgments

I would like to express my heartfelt gratitude to the many people who have contributed to this book's creation. First and foremost, I want to thank my family for their love, patience, and constant support. Special thanks to my wife Namrata for motivating me to write this book. To my little son Dhrutav, your joy, and curiosity inspire me every day. This book is as much yours as it is mine; your love and presence make everything I do so much more meaningful.

A huge thank you to my teammates Vaibhav, Anuja, and Tanushri whose collaboration and dedication were vital throughout this journey. Your hard work, enthusiasm, and support made every step of this process more enjoyable. This project wouldn't have been possible without your contributions.

Lastly, to my students, thank you for inspiring me to write a book on this topic and for helping me recognize the need for a practical guide in market research. Your support and feedback have been invaluable, and I hope the pages of this book provide something meaningful to you. This journey wouldn't have been as rewarding without your encouragement.

I hope this book serves as a valuable resource, and I look forward to the continued learning and growth it brings. Thank you everyone for being a part of this valuable experience.

Market Research Awakening: A Student's Journey

Meet Dhrutav, a college student who after a long day of lectures, was in desperate need of a break. His brain was screaming for some rest, so, he made his way to the cafeteria for a cup of coffee. As he stood in line, he noticed a huge banner announcing the launch of a new "exclusive" coffee blend.

"Try our new premium roast, refuel yourself in 10 mins!" it boldly declared.

At first, Dhrutav was intrigued and amazed. Just a few days ago, he had been talking with his friends about discovering a new coffee flavor, and now here it was, right in front of him. It felt almost unreal. Was this really happening, or was he dreaming he thought?

*..itni shiddat se maine tumhe paane ki **coffee-ish** ki hai, ki har zarre ne mujhe tumse milane ki saazish ki hai..* 😆 😆

But then, a thought crossed his mind: Who had conspired to make this coffee? Was it his own desperate need for caffeine, or had someone, somewhere, somehow figured out exactly what he was craving for?

It didn't take long for Dhrutav to realize what was going on. Someone had made a strategic decision to create this coffee blend, marketed it to stressed-out, and tired students like him, and made it sound like a perfect solution to their boredom, and lethargy.

But how did they know exactly what he wanted?

11

And that he would spend over $5 on a cup of coffee instead of sticking to his usual $2 brew?

That, my friend, is the magic of market research at work.

Now, you might be thinking, "So what? Dhrutav was buying a cup of coffee—no big deal!"

But that's the point: market research is everywhere, and it's influencing most of the decisions we make every day, often without us even realizing it. It's why we opt for that pricey cup of coffee instead of an affordable one, and why we're irresistibly drawn to the latest smartphone model that promises unique differentiating features with smart marketing doing the rest.

Market research, in its simplest form, is about gathering, analyzing, and interpreting data to understand what people want, what they don't, and why. Think of it like being a detective, but instead of solving crimes, you're figuring out what people want. You're putting together clues to understand why something as simple as a cup of coffee feels like the best choice for your day (Like Dhrutav did!)

Pretty clever, right?

Well, that's the power of market research.

It's happening all around you, shaping your choices each day and every day!

Now, let's break it down:

The Market: The coffee market here refers to key stakeholders such as coffee producers, manufacturers, retailers, distributors, cafes, and customers.

The Market Players: All coffee manufacturers, coffee shop chains, and even campus vending machines, that serve customers their trendy drinks, limited-period offers, and customizable options.

The Consumers: The students, professionals, and coffee enthusiasts who crave more than just a caffeine kick; they desire an experience that feels personalized to their preferences.

Market research connects these key parts: the market, the players in it, and the customers. By analyzing the market trends, competitors, and customer needs, market research gives businesses a clear picture of the current market situation. This interconnected approach helps businesses make informed decisions, explore untapped opportunities, and draft competitive strategies that resonate with customer needs, ultimately driving success in a competitive market.

Curiosity Unleashed

Market research isn't just some fancy buzzword or a random subject you have to sit through. It's the secret sauce behind many decisions we make every day without giving much thought to it. From the products we buy to the ads that pop up everywhere and even the courses we pick (because flipping a coin didn't seem like a solid career plan!). It's like the invisible hand directing all our choices and telling us what to do!

Resuming our coffee story,

That's when Dhrutav decided to take the plunge and explore this field in depth. He was fascinated by how businesses made these seemingly small yet game-changing decisions. How did they crack the code of knowing what people wanted—even before we knew it ourselves? He couldn't help but wonder, *Could I learn to crack the code of markets—not just for coffee, but for anything?*

You see what happened in this story. It all started with Dhrutav's curiosity to question "How has someone figured out his need for a particular coffee variant?"

I'm sure many readers in the market research industry can relate to Dhrutav's story. It reminds me of an experience from my first internship when I was tasked with analyzing consumer behavior in snack selections at stores. Visiting a few convenience stores and observing numerous customers, I began to notice a distinct pattern: some brands were consistently chosen, while others were left behind. This sparked a question that kept running through my mind: *What made one product so appealing while another was overlooked? Was it the price, the packaging, or something entirely different?*

That seemingly simple assignment became my gateway into the fascinating world of market research. It wasn't just about selling; it was about understanding people and creating solutions for their needs—something that fascinated me. This was my first encounter with market research, and it lit a spark that eventually turned into a full-fledged passion. Over the years, this journey has been one of discovery—learning the tools, mastering the techniques, and seeing the real-world impact of strategic research.

Now, fast forward to today, and I'm here, eager to share everything I've learned. This book is my way of answering those initial questions and showing you how market research can be your superpower, no matter what field you're exploring!

In this book, you'll learn how to ask those same questions and find answers using market research. We'll dive into the concepts and strategies that will allow you to understand and navigate the world of market research with confidence. Together, we'll learn the tools and techniques, master the art of spotting trends, and uncover how to turn data into smart business decisions. It's not just about coffee or products, it's about understanding the world around us and how everything is linked through thoughtful, systematic research. I'll provide you with a clear, step-by-step action plan, offering practical advice on how to prepare and succeed in the market research industry. My goal is to inspire you to take control of your path and step boldly into the future you've imagined for yourself.

So, grab your curiosity and your sense of adventure because this journey is just getting started!

Market Research: Powering Business Success

Imagine launching a spaceship without a destination in mind; pretty reckless, right? That's what businesses risk doing when they skip market research. In today's fast-paced world, where trends shift quicker than a toddler changes his mind, market research serves as a strategic compass, guiding companies through the complex landscape of dynamic consumer needs, growing competition, and the latest emerging technology. Market research is no longer a luxury for businesses; it has become a crucial element and the key differentiator between a thriving business and one that merely survives. In this rapidly changing world, it's not just about having a great product, it's about knowing when and how to deliver it.

Let's look at a few examples to put things into perspective. Coca-Cola launched Coke Zero after studying the growing demand for low-calorie drinks, which allowed them to attract health-conscious consumers while retaining their loyal customer base. Likewise, Netflix used data-driven market research to predict the success of shows like *Stranger Things*, capitalizing on nostalgia and the popularity of sci-fi content.

Importance of Market Research and Why You Should Know About It

Imagine you're designing a new app, pitching a business idea, or even leading a group project. Without market research, it's like throwing darts blindfolded, hoping to hit the bullseye. It's not just about knowing what people want, it's about understanding *why* they want it. Whether it's a marketing class or an entrepreneurship project, mastering market research gives your ideas direction, impact, and relevance.

Beyond the classroom, market research sets you apart in the professional world. Employers value candidates who can decode trends, analyze consumer behavior, and provide actionable insights. It's a skill that turns you into the go-to person for solving real-world business challenges. Imagine being the one in a meeting who can confidently answer, "What do customers want?" or predict the next big thing. That's not just valuable—it's game-changing.

Why Think About a Career in Market Research?

Before we jump into why market research might be the career choice for you, let's take a step back and think about what makes a job your "dream job." What are the qualities that would make you excited to wake up and dive into your work every day? Whether it's opportunities for growth, meaningful impact, or a balanced lifestyle, identifying what you truly want from your career will help you determine if market research is the perfect fit for you. Let's take this time to explore your career aspirations and see how this dynamic field could bring you closer to that dream job you've been thinking.

What Do You Expect from Your Dream Job?

Let's be honest; when most people think about their dream job, it's not just about the paycheck (though, we all know it's important!). It's about feeling inspired and motivated by the work, having room to grow professionally, and achieving a balance between career and personal life. It's about being able to make a meaningful impact while enjoying the perks that come with a successful career.

Here are the top things that most people seek in their dream job;

☑ Excitement and variety in their daily tasks.

☑ Financial stability and opportunities for growth.

☑ Flexibility to manage both work and personal life.

☑ The chance to make a real difference in their industry or community.

Now, here's the burning question: Does market research provide all of this? Spoiler alert: Absolutely, it does!

Market research is one of those fields that checks all the boxes when it comes to what most people dream of in a job. First off, it offers intellectual stimulation with diverse and challenging projects that keep you engaged ☑ . Every day presents new trends, and data, keeping the work dynamic and exciting. Whether you're analyzing consumer behavior or tracking industry shifts, the variety is endless. It's not just about crunching numbers, this job puts you in the driver's seat to shape strategies, drive decisions, and even influence product development.

Financial rewards? Check! ✅

Market research professionals are highly sought after, with lucrative salary prospects and clear growth opportunities. Companies rely on market research to stay competitive, meaning there's always demand for skilled professionals. Moreover, the skills you build are transferable, offering flexibility to move across industries or roles.

And let's not forget work-life balance.

Many market research roles offer the flexibility of remote work, flexible hours, and the opportunity to work across various time zones, giving you the freedom to balance your personal life with your career. ✅

Finally, impact!

Market research helps businesses understand their customers, make better decisions, and innovate, giving you the chance to make a meaningful difference in how companies serve their clients or shape their products. ✅

So, if you're looking for a career that combines excitement, growth, flexibility, and the opportunity to make a real impact, market research might just be the dream job you're searching for. 🔍 🔍

Why should this matter to you?

As we've already touched on, market research has the potential to be your dream career. But wait, there's more! Let me share some compelling reasons why you should seriously consider diving into the world of market research. Trust me, you've got to see it to believe it – this field offers opportunities and excitement that might just surprise you! Keep reading to discover why market research could be your next big career move; one that will make you think, "I wish I'd jumped in earlier!"

India's Dynamic Consumer Landscape

India isn't just a country—it's a vibrant, ever-changing mosaic of consumer preferences that constantly shifts and evolves. With a population of 1.4 billion, spread across diverse regions, languages, and cultural flavors, it's a market that constantly keeps you on your toes. What's a hot trend in Mumbai might fall flat in Chennai, and what's buzzing in Bangalore could be a total miss in Patna.

Market research in India is like being on an endless treasure hunt. With new preferences, buying behaviors, and trends popping up constantly, there's always something new to discover. As a market researcher, you're like a decoder, solving the mystery of why Gen Z can't get enough of one sneaker brand while millennials are hooked on another. You'll be the one predicting trend before they go viral, giving brands the upper hand in crafting strategies that resonate with India's diverse audience. And with India's ever-evolving market, there is a growing need for "troubleshooters" like you to stay ahead of the game. Sounds exciting, doesn't it?

A Booming Industry with Boundless Potential

Let's dive into the numbers for a second, the global market research industry is expected to surpass $105 billion by 2028. That's right, BILLION, with a capital B . And what does that mean for you? Well, it's a clear signal that the demand for data-driven insights is skyrocketing, and the momentum isn't slowing down anytime soon.

While other industries may face fluctuations or slowdowns, market research continues to witness consistent growth. I know you would be wondering about the reason behind my optimistic prediction. I get that!

Market research isn't tied to the performance of any single industry; rather, it plays a critical role in the decision-making processes across all sectors 🌐 . This broad applicability is what fuels the ongoing upward trajectory of the market research industry. If you have an analytical mindset, a knack for identifying patterns, and a curiosity for discovering insights, market research is calling your name. With the industry growing at a rapid pace, there are endless opportunities for you to carve out a rewarding career path.

Diverse Opportunities Across the Country

India's market research industry is booming, and it's not concentrated in a particular location similar to what we have for a few other sectors like manufacturing and IT services. There are over a thousand market research firms spread across the country, opportunities are as diverse as the cities themselves. You always have a choice to pick a company that's conveniently located near you. Whether you're in a bustling city or a quieter spot, there's a market research company trying to make its global impact.

Market research offers a diverse range of opportunities across sectors, making it an exciting field for anyone with sector-specific interests. Whether you're eager to impact the future of healthcare, dive into the fast-paced world of technology, or shape consumer trends in the FMCG sector, there's a niche for every passion. The best part? You get to choose the industry that sparks your curiosity and drives your excitement!

Gateway to Strategic Consulting

If you've ever dreamt of working for elite consulting firms like McKinsey, BCG, or Bain, guess what? Market research might just be your golden ticket! These prestigious companies thrive on individuals who can dissect data, identify emerging trends, and think strategically. The very same skills that are at the core of market research.

Starting your career in market research is like getting a front-row seat in the world of business strategy. You'll be building and nurturing all the skills that top consulting firms look for in a prospective candidate. Market research doesn't just help you meet expectations; it equips you to exceed them. When you're ready to dive into the consulting world, you'll have a wealth of skills that position you as the strategist these top firms are eager to find. Ready to turn your passion for data into a game-changing career? This is where it all begins.

Flexibility and Independence

Let's be honest: the typical 9-to-5 office routine isn't for everyone. Some thrive in the hustle, while others crave the freedom to pursue their passions on their own terms. As a skilled researcher, you can handpick the projects that get your adrenaline pumping. Whether you're consulting for a Fortune 500 brand or analyzing the next big thing in indie tech, market research adapts to your lifestyle; not the other way around.

You're in control of when and how you work. You can set your schedule, work from anywhere, and focus on the projects that fuel your passion. Whether it's a global brand or a niche market, you're calling the shots. It's the dream career for anyone who values independence and flexibility to navigate their career.

Fosters Diversity and Inclusion

Market research stands out as one of the few industries where diverse backgrounds aren't just welcomed but are truly celebrated. Businesses are in constant search for individuals who can bring cross-industry expertise and innovative solutions to the table. Whether your background is in engineering, design, healthcare, or the arts, your unique perspective can make a significant impact, as long as you bring strong analytical and research skills to the mix.

A market research career also offers an exceptionally flexible path for those returning after a career break. Unlike many industries that frown upon career gaps, market research embraces the reality that life events are a part of everyone's journey. Whether you took time off for personal reasons, family, or travel, your skills are always in demand. This industry values talent over timelines, empowering you to resume your career and pick up right from where you left off.

International Career Prospects

The demand for skilled market researchers is not confined to one country or region; in fact, it spans across the globe. Whether you're working for a multinational corporation, a local firm with global clients, or as a consultant, the skills you develop are universally recognized.

The market research industry also offers opportunities to collaborate with international teams, giving you the chance to work cross-culturally and build a globally diverse skill set. If you've ever dreamed of living and working in places like London, Singapore, or Dubai, market research could be your ticket to an international career. ⊕

Closing thoughts

The market research industry is experiencing promising growth, and the career opportunities are endless. Whether you come from any academic background, market research acknowledges and welcomes your analytical skills. This makes it an ideal career for those looking to switch industries or return to work after a break. It's a field that thrives on diverse insights from different industries helping businesses make critical decisions.

What makes market research even more exciting is its adaptability. As industries evolve and technology advances, especially with AI, robotics, and automation, market researchers are always at the forefront, uncovering trends and helping companies stay ahead of the competition. In this fast-paced environment, you'll continuously sharpen your skills and expand your expertise. Whether you're working on global projects or diving into specialized sectors, market research offers unmatched flexibility and growth. If you're looking for a career that challenges you, sparks innovation, and offers several growth opportunities, market research might be the perfect fit for you.

Market Research Analyst- The Business Detective

Behind every successful business strategy lies the expertise of a market research analyst, the unsung hero who decodes customer preferences,

predicts emerging trends, and guides companies toward making informed decisions to stay ahead of the competition. These professionals transform raw data into actionable

insights, shaping how businesses evolve in ever-changing markets. Curious about what a market research analyst truly does? Let's dive into a real-world example to uncover their critical role in driving business success.

Case Study: Choosing an eco-friendly product

You're the proud owner of your area's leading coffee shop chain. Just picture it—let yourself feel it too! 🕴️ 🙂

The Coffee business is booming, and customers are lining up for their daily dose of caffeine, but there's a challenge. Competition is seriously heating up these days. Lately, you've been hearing chatter about customers consciously seeking more sustainable options by reducing plastic and embracing more eco-friendly materials. It's like everyone's having a "Coffee pe Charcha"

But how can you tell if this is just a fad or a real shift in consumer behavior? That's where your secret Santa comes in: the market research analyst.

You bring in an analyst to help you out. The first thing the analyst does? Dives straight into the data. He sends out surveys, sorts through customer feedback, and digs into industry reports on sustainability trends in the food and beverages market. He even takes a look at what the competitors are up to and checks out their eco-friendly launches and sales numbers for the last couple of months.

After all, numbers don't lie. (I remember a song here)

Ok let's get back to this case and see what Shakira analyzes ... I am talking about the analyst we hired to solve this case! Tum log bhi na??

Well, turns out that 60% of your customers prefer biodegradable cups, and 75% would be happy to pay 10% more for sustainable products. Now that's some useful info!

Well done, Shakira!

Armed with these insights, you can confidently decide whether it's time to ditch the plastic and switch to eco-friendly packaging or ramp up your marketing efforts to highlight your sustainable brand image. It was all about making smart choices, and now you've got the roadmap.

But wait, there's more! A market research analyst doesn't just report on what's happening right now. They're also on the lookout for what's coming next. Could it be plant-based milk alternatives? Maybe AI-powered coffee makers? Who knows, but that's where the analyst's magic comes in. We'll dive into how analysts spot emerging trends in the next chapter. For now, let's chat about the must-have skills for the market research analyst.

Market Research Analyst – Skills as Superpowers

Imagine a world where every business decision relies on uncovering the secrets hidden in data. From predicting trends to understanding the "why" behind customer choices, this field blends creativity with logic, curiosity with strategy, and analysis with storytelling. At the center of it is the market research analyst, a modern-day star who navigates the sea of information to guide businesses toward success.

But being a market research analyst isn't just about gazing at spreadsheets or flipping through reports (though there's plenty of that too! 🤩). It's about mastering a set of super skills that help you turn numbers into insights and data into decisions.

Research Skills – The Fact-Finding Work 🕵️

In market research, strong research skills are the foundation of success. Without them, tackling the challenges of the business world is like trying to find your way through a dense fog without a compass. It's not enough to simply gather data; the real value lies in what you do with it. Research skills help you dig deeper, uncovering the patterns, trends, and stories hidden within these patterns.

Every piece of information has a story to tell, and it's the researcher's job to bring that story to light. Whether it's identifying customer preferences, or analyzing competitor strategies, strong research skills enable you to connect the dots and reveal the bigger picture. This is what transforms raw information into actionable insights that drive smart decisions.

Analytical Skills – The Number Cruncher 🖥️

Imagine you are looking at a spreadsheet filled with sales numbers, and there's a sudden spike. At first glance, it may seem like a success, but the analyst's job is to go beyond it. The market research analyst needs to figure out *why* it happened. Is it tied to a seasonal trend, a new marketing campaign, or a change in customer behavior?

To get to the bottom of the real cause for this spike, he would dive into additional data on customer reviews, industry reports, marketing performance metrics, and competitor activity. Analyzing data isn't just about crunching numbers; it's about discovering the story hidden within them. The market research analyst has a challenge in solving the puzzle where the pieces don't always fit perfectly 🧩 🧩 , but his analytical skills can bring them together to form a clear picture.

Technical Skills – The Gadget Geek 🖥️

Technical tools allow the analyst to unlock deeper layers of data, streamline processes, and make complex information digestible. These skills empower him to tackle big datasets with confidence, reveal hidden patterns, and present your findings in a way that leaves a lasting impression.

When tasked with presenting evolving sales trends to your team, the analyst prepares an interactive Tableau dashboard instead of old-school bar charts. Suddenly, data becomes dynamic, engaging, and easy to explore. The user of the dashboard now can filter by region, compare product performance, and identify patterns with just a click. It's like upgrading from your vintage car to a Ferrari - 🚗 😃

Finance Skills – The Numbers Whisperer 💰

In the world of business, financial reports are more than just numbers on a page, they're like treasure maps that reveal hidden insights. Imagine yourself as a financial investigator, analyzing data clues to reveal the full story. Is the company growing stronger, or are profits starting to slip? Are expenses getting out of hand, or is there a smart investment strategy in motion? Every number has a story to tell, and your job is to figure it out and understand what it really means for the business.

Each financial figure whether it's a percentage increase in revenue or a jump in operating costs holds valuable clues. Your job is to look beyond the surface and interpret what these numbers truly mean, connecting the dots to understand the company's overall financial story.

Business Writing & Communication Skills — The People Person

As a market research analyst, you might be surprised to discover how much writing you'll be doing. It's not all spreadsheets and charts, you'll be churning out reports, presentations, and summaries that require more than just your analytical brainpower.

Don't worry! Writing clearly and concisely will soon feel effortless. After all, the last thing you want is for your clients to fall asleep while reading your insights -

As an analyst, you'll often interact with clients, stakeholders, and customers, keeping them engaged by presenting compelling and impactful narratives. Mastering both writing and communication skills will elevate you from an analyst to a trusted leader and storyteller, enabling you to create a lasting impact on the business.

Building Your Online Presence: A Must for Job Seekers

Why is it so Important?

In today's world, your online presence is your digital introduction. It shows up before you do at the upcoming networking event. It's like your virtual self is already at the party 😎, stealing the spotlight while you're still figuring out which shoes to wear 😶

Whether it's a potential employer, a future client, or an old colleague, what they see online is usually the first thing that forms their opinion about you. Whether it's a polished LinkedIn profile, an insightful blog, or an active Twitter feed, your digital footprint tells a story. In this fast-paced, tech-driven world, that story can either open doors of opportunity or leave them closed.

So, take a moment and ask yourself: how's your online story shaping up? Is it telling the narrative you want the world to see, or is it time for a digital refresh?

Showcase Your Skills and Achievements

Your online presence on platforms like LinkedIn or a personal portfolio website serves as your virtual stage, offering you the chance to stand out and shine. Think of them as your digital resume with the bonus of being able to showcase what you've actually done. It's your opportunity to display everything from successful projects to certifications, and even the smaller wins that reflect your dedication.

These platforms help you go beyond the standard resume with bullet points and allow you to present your skills more dynamically. You can highlight the challenges you faced, the innovative solutions you applied, the key "aha" moments, the lessons learned, and the meaningful impact of your work.

Build a Powerful Network

Building a strong network online presence is not about sending invites and collecting connections, it's about forging meaningful relationships with industry leaders, mentors, and peers who can open doors to new opportunities. By making the right impression online, you can easily reach out to professionals in your field and start conversations that could lead to collaborations, partnerships, or even career-changing advice.

Moreover, having a well-curated online profile increases your chances of being discovered by employers and recruiters who are constantly searching for new talent. Companies are increasingly looking beyond resumes and conducting online searches to find candidates who fit their needs. Whether you're actively hunting for a job or browsing to keep your options open, maintaining an engaging online presence ensures you stay relevant and visible for the next opportunity that comes your way.

Stand Out in Competitive Market

The job market today is more competitive than ever, with applications for each open position increasing year after year. For hiring managers, the sheer volume of resumes can be overwhelming, leading them to rely on automated software for initial screenings. These tools are designed to scrutinize applications and highlight those that feature standout qualities, making it more important than ever to **Differentiate Yourself.**

This is where a compelling online presence becomes a game-changer. It goes beyond the resume, acting as a dynamic showcase of your unique skills, experiences, and professional brand. When recruiters discover you online, they see more than just qualifications. They see the differentiating qualities that make you an ideal candidate. A strong online profile clearly conveys that you are proactive, professional, and ready to face challenges with confidence.

The LinkedIn Blueprint for Success

Building a strong LinkedIn profile is essential for establishing your professional online presence and opening doors to a wide range of career opportunities. In today's digital age, your LinkedIn profile is often the first impression potential employers, collaborators, or clients have of you. A well-crafted profile serves as your professional resume while also highlighting your personality, interests, and online engagement.

Here's how to use it effectively:

Build a Killer Profile

Building a killer LinkedIn profile is your first step toward making a lasting impression in the professional world. Kick things off with a professional photo that acts as your first virtual introduction creating a lasting impression. A clear, friendly, and polished headshot instantly establishes credibility and makes your profile more approachable. Profiles with photos are much more likely to be viewed, so skip the vacation selfies and invest in a professional picture with a smile -

Next, craft a catchy headline that grabs the viewer's attention. This isn't just your job title; it's your personal elevator pitch. Instead of "Software Engineer," go for something like, *"Innovative Software Engineer | Building Scalable Solutions with a Passion for Problem-Solving."* Your headline is one of the first things people see, so make it memorable and reflective of your unique value. Think of it as the hook that encourages people to dive deeper into your profile.

ProTip

"Choose 5 keywords that best define you, add some style & elegance, and voilà—your headline is good to go!"

Next, you add some substance by showcasing your education, skills, and achievements. Elaborate on your qualifications, certifications, and any projects that highlight your expertise. Whether it's a degree from a prestigious university or a skill you've honed through practical experience, each addition strengthens your profile. Use bullet points, quantifiable results, and clear descriptions to make your accomplishments pop. This is your chance to tell your professional story and prove why you stand out from the crowd. When done right, your profile evolves from just a page into a powerful representation of your personal brand!

Engage with Content

Engaging on LinkedIn by sharing posts, commenting on industry news, and writing about your experiences are your ways of saying, "Hey, I'm here, and I've got something interesting to contribute!" The more you engage, the more visible and relatable you become to your network and beyond.

Start by sharing posts that not only resonate with your field but also reflect your personal journey and professional experiences. Whether it's about a challenging project you've recently tackled or a breakthrough moment that shaped your career, don't be afraid to dive into your story. People connect with real experiences, so if you've overcome obstacles or learned valuable lessons along the way, share them! Offering insights from your latest project can spark interesting conversations and help you position yourself as a thought leader in your space.

Instead of simply consuming information, be an active participant. Share your thoughts, join discussions, or offer advice. The beauty of LinkedIn lies in its community-driven nature, your next post or comment could be the spark that leads to a meaningful connection, or an unexpected opportunity. So, get out there, share your experiences, and watch your network grow!

ProTip

Consistent engagement boosts your visibility to recruiters and builds meaningful connections. Comment thoughtfully on industry posts, share insights, and establish your expertise with regular, impactful content.

Use Keywords

Using the right keywords on your LinkedIn profile is like setting up a guidepost that leads people directly to you. It ensures recruiters and opportunities locate you effortlessly. If your profile isn't optimized, you're like a shop with no signboard - 😑

Optimizing your profile with the right keywords is more than just a strategy; it's about aligning your skills and experience with the exact terms recruiters are searching for. Think of it as speaking the same language as the person who's hiring. As I mentioned earlier, recruiters don't have time to go through every resume; it's like searching for a needle in a haystack! 😅

Instead, they rely on specific keywords to filter through the sea of applications and pinpoint the best candidates quickly. That's where the SEO magic happens, helping you stand out and get noticed! (More on SEO some other time, maybe next edition of this book - 🤓 😇)

Pro Tip

Take a look at the job postings of your interest and notice the words that pop up repeatedly. For instance, "data analysis," "consumer insights," or "trend forecasting," for a market research analyst job. Sprinkle those terms into your profile naturally. And yes, naturally is key, don't just list every tool or skill you've ever Googled 👣 👣

Network Intentionally

Networking intentionally on LinkedIn is like navigating a crowded room at a professional event to cultivate genuine, lasting relationships that can truly enhance your career. You can consciously position yourself to connect with people who share similar interests, goals, and values and start striking meaningful conversations with them.

Intentional networking fosters trust, and credibility, and opens the door to countless opportunities, whether it's finding a mentor, learning from others, or even landing your next big job.

Send personalized connection requests, engage in meaningful conversations, share your thoughts in comments, and seek advice to build genuine relationships. Start with Alumni and Colleagues!

Mastering Trends: Shaping the Future of Business

Welcome to the world of trends, where spotting the next big thing is your secret recipe for staying ahead in the game. Trends are like ocean waves. Some are large and visible from a distance, while others are subtle and catch you by surprise when they roll in. Identifying trends is crucial for every business to make informed decisions, whether it's a global movement, a regional shift, or a seasonal spark. So, how do you become a proficient trend-spotter? Well, you don't need a magic wand here, you need to be just someone who's a wizard at Googling!

The art of identifying trends starts with a curious mind. Ask yourself, "What's changing in my industry? In my community? In the world?" A trend often gets created around us as a whisper, gaining momentum until it becomes a shout. Social media, for example, is like the cafeteria of the internet, full of chatter, and reels. From hashtags to viral videos, platforms like Instagram, TikTok, and LinkedIn are filled with emerging ideas waiting to break into the global trends.

Trends aren't always the ones shouting for attention; sometimes, they're more like the quiet person at a party who drops the wisdom bomb. Take the surge in demand for eco-friendly materials in fashion, it's not just about looking stylish; it's about saving the planet from a mountain of plastic and landfill disasters. Who would have imagined a few decades ago that making sustainable choices to save the Earth would become the hottest trend?

The shift in fashion has gained momentum, with its impact being felt by luxury brands and leading fashion giants. Today's consumers, particularly younger generations, are not only focused on looking good but are also making conscious and informed decisions. From recycled fabrics to clothing rental services, the fashion industry is evolving in response to the growing demand for sustainability. What began as a quiet change has now turned into a powerful movement, signalling that this trend is here to stay and will redefine the future of the fashion industry!

To spot these deeper trends, you need to dive in headfirst and immerse yourself in industry reports, surveys, and articles from thought leaders. These sources provide valuable data and insights, but that's just the beginning. To truly understand the dynamics of a trend, you've got to get out there and *talk* to people. Engage with your customers, chat with colleagues, or even ask your friendly neighborhood barista about the latest buzz. Sometimes, the best insights may come from casual conversations or unexpected sources. People love to share their opinions, whether it's about a new product, a shift in their habits, or their expectations for the future. So, don't focus solely on the numbers; pay attention to the voices around you. You'd be surprised by how a casual conversation can

spark the next big trend. Remember, every groundbreaking idea probably began with someone saying, 'What if we did this?' and someone else saying, 'That's ridiculous!' and Boom 💣 …, a trend is born."

Spotting a trend is just half the battle. Recognizing a shift and responding to it with the right strategies, products, or services is where the magic lies. A crucial question to consider is: are you ready to embrace the emerging trend on the horizon? Can you reinvent your offerings, adjust your strategy, or even rethink your business model to stay ahead of what's coming next? History shows that those who capture the trend earlier often become the leaders of their industry. Take the pioneers of e-commerce as an example; what started as a bold move to bring shopping online turned companies like Amazon and Alibaba into global giants. They didn't just spot the trend; they built entire empires around it. 🏭

So, don't be a passive observer. Dive in, experiment, and see how you can make a trend work for you. Test your ideas, gather feedback, and refine your approach. Trends aren't just opportunities; they're invitations to innovate and grow. The ones who accept the challenge with agility and creativity are the ones who turn potential into realized business opportunities.

Here's another interesting insight about trends; they're not just for businesses or brands trying to stay competitive. On a personal level, staying aware of trends can give you a competitive edge in remaining relevant in an ever-evolving world. Whether it's learning a new skill, mastering the latest technology, or updating your wardrobe to stay ahead in the style game, trends provide opportunities to grow and reinvent yourself.

Think about it, learning to navigate emerging tools like AI or blockchain today could make you a pioneer in tomorrow's workplace. Exploring new career paths, such as becoming a social media influencer, might ignite passions you never knew existed. And yes, staying ahead of fashion trends could make you the trendsetter in your social circle.

The next time you come across something intriguing, a new app, an exciting idea, or even a quirky TikTok challenge—don't dismiss it as just a passing trend. Take a closer look, explore its possibilities, and see how it aligns with your journey. Who knows? That seemingly small

step could spark a major transformation. Trends aren't just fleeting moments; they're windows into the future, offering you the chance to evolve, adapt, and shine.

Types of Trends? – Real Game Changers

At its core, a trend is simply a pattern, a direction in which something is heading. It's what's buzzing right now, or even more exciting, what's about to buzz tomorrow. Think of trends as the taste buds of the business world—they help you figure out what people are craving, often before they even realize it themselves. Understanding trends isn't just about keeping up; it's about anticipating what's next and being ready to ride the wave.

Trends come in all shapes and sizes, and here are some key types to keep on your radar:

Global Trends

Global trends are the powerful waves that ripple across continents, reshaping how societies function, industries evolve, and individuals adapt . They're universal forces that redefine the way we live, work, and connect. Imagine them as the tectonic plates of the trend world, shifting and creating shockwaves that touch everything from consumer habits to business strategies. Look at the impact of Artificial Intelligence on the world. It has gone from being a futuristic concept to an integral part of our daily lives, reshaping how we work, shop, and interact.

Take OpenAI's ChatGPT as an example . It has transformed communication and content creation by providing a sophisticated AI tool capable of generating human-like text with remarkable accuracy. For individuals, it simplifies tasks like writing emails, creating social media posts, and brainstorming ideas. For businesses, ChatGPT streamlines customer service, enhances marketing efforts, and improves productivity by automating repetitive content generation. This widespread adoption has helped ChatGPT become a global trend, highlighting AI's transformative potential in shaping how we interact, work, and create content across multiple sectors.

Regional Trends

Regional trends are movements or behaviors that emerge in specific geographic locations and are initially embraced by local communities, cultures, or subgroups. These trends often reflect the unique characteristics, values, or interests of that region. This could be anything from a local food trend, fashion style, or even a new social behavior that resonates with people. When people in one region see something interesting, they may start to adopt it, and it becomes a global trend. ✂ ✂ Regional trends are not just fleeting fads, they reflect the ever-

evolving dynamics of culture and society, demonstrating how local interests, with the right timing, exposure, and influence, can rapidly grow into global movements.

Have you ever heard of Bubble Tea? … No, it's not the same as Bubble gum 😬 🫧

Bubble tea, the delightful Taiwanese drink known for its chewy tapioca pearls and customizable flavors, has evolved well beyond its modest origins. However, its most passionate following may just be found in Tokyo. While the drink originally made waves across Asia, Tokyo has embraced it in a way that goes beyond just a trend to become a cultural phenomenon. With its endless combinations of flavors, textures, and colors, bubble tea in Tokyo has transformed into a fun, social experience that people of all ages are eagerly embracing.

In the bustling streets of Tokyo, you can find bubble tea café's on nearly every street corner, each offering something unique that makes your drink as fun to look at as it is to sip. As more and more people across the world discovered the joy of chewy pearls and endless flavor possibilities, bubble tea's global reach began to expand. What was once a local favourite has now become a global trend, with cities like New York, London, and Sydney eagerly embracing it.

Just like Tokyo embraced bubble tea as its own , cities across the world are discovering the joy of this playful, customizable drink. It's a perfect example of how a regional trend can start small, create a massive local impact, and eventually ripple out to influence the global market, transforming a niche offering into a worldwide sensation.

Seasonal Trends

Seasonal trends are like switching out your wardrobe to match the time of year, just as you wouldn't wear shorts in the middle of winter or a jacket during a summer heatwave, these trends are shaped by the seasons. From fashion to food, fitness to entertainment, seasonal trends spark excitement tied to specific months of the calendar. 🍁 🌿

While they may only last for a short period, their power to capture attention and boost sales makes them a key player in the world of trends. After all, when it comes to seasonal trends, timing is everything!

Let us talk about a familiar seasonal trend that most of us have witnessed sometime in our lives. When the New Year rolls around, a lot of us head towards the gym inspired by our New Year's resolutions to get fit 💪 💪 .

It's a classic case of a trend born out of seasonality. People are motivated by the idea of a fresh start and the promise of a healthier year.

The trick for gyms is recognizing that this seasonal spike is inevitable, and it's about harnessing that burst of motivation during the New Year rush. To maintain momentum, gym owners develop engaging programs and promotions that keep new members focused, converting their initial enthusiasm into lasting change.

Technological Trends

Technological trends are the driving force behind some of the most significant shifts in our world. Whether it's a revolutionary new tool that changes the way we live or a groundbreaking development that redefines industries, technology is constantly pushing boundaries and opening doors to new possibilities. In recent years, we've witnessed some mind-bending innovations like blockchain, quantum computing, and the rise of artificial intelligence (AI), all of which have disrupted traditional business models and created entirely new markets. These advancements don't just make things faster or more efficient, they change the way we think about problems and solutions.

One such tech is the home automation gadgets that allow people to control everything from lighting to security systems with just the touch of a button. Companies like Google and Amazon have capitalized on this trend, creating ecosystems of interconnected products that make  our homes smarter and more efficient. As the Internet of Things (IoT) continues to expand, we're seeing even more integration between devices, further simplifying our lives and offering businesses new opportunities to innovate.

Social and Cultural Trends

Social and cultural trends show us what people care about and how their values and lifestyles are changing. These trends illustrate the powerful forces at play in shaping modern society, highlighting the growing importance of values like inclusivity, well-being, and mindfulness, which guide consumer behavior and expectations. 🛍️

The growing trend of "pet parenting," especially in urban and suburban areas, is driving lifestyle changes such as smaller families, delayed marriages, and increased urbanization. In countries like the United States and Japan, where individualism is growing, pets play a crucial role in filling emotional voids and providing unconditional love and companionship 🐕. Meanwhile, in India, a traditionally family-centric culture, pets are becoming an integral part of households, celebrated in festivals like *Kukur Tihar* in Nepal, where dogs are honored for their loyalty and companionship. The increasing cultural acceptance of pets has created ripple effects across various industries.

From pet-friendly travel accommodations to luxury pet spas and even pet influencer marketing, the bond between humans and animals is shaping everything from business strategies to digital culture. Embracing pet companionship goes beyond being just a lifestyle choice; it embodies values such as empathy, connection, and responsibility. This cultural shift is not only reshaping how people view pets but also influencing business ecosystems, highlighting how these changes affect the nature of businesses across industries. From pet services to pet-related products, the growing emphasis on pet parenting is creating new market opportunities and altering consumer behavior. 🐱 🚀

Economic Trends

Economic trends are like hidden forces that shape the way businesses and industries grow. They impact how people make and spend money and push companies to adapt and innovate. Whether it's the rise of freelance work in the gig economy, the growing popularity of cryptocurrencies, or changes in how consumers shop, these trends highlight new opportunities and challenges, helping industries stay relevant in an ever-evolving world.

Did you dare to a world where money isn't tied to banks or borders a few decades ago? Welcome to the era of cryptocurrency. Once dismissed as a niche idea, digital currencies like Bitcoin and Ethereum have sparked a financial revolution. Countries like El Salvador

adopting Bitcoin as legal tender show how economic trends can blur the lines between innovation and policy. From transforming payment systems to revolutionizing industries through blockchain technology, cryptocurrencies are not just an economic trend, they're a global force reshaping the future.

Industry-Specific Trends

Industry-specific trends are the driving forces that define how individual sectors evolve, innovate, and respond to challenges. Unlike broader trends, these are deeply rooted in the unique needs, technologies, and dynamics of specific fields. Staying attuned to these movements not only helps businesses stay relevant but also allows them to lead change within their domain.

The shift towards **electric vehicles (EVs)** is a clear example of an industry-specific trend reshaping an entire sector. Companies like Tesla, Rivian, and even legacy automakers like Ford and GM are investing heavily in EV technology to meet the growing demand for sustainable transportation. The push for EVs has also spurred advancements in battery technology and charging infrastructure, creating ripple effects across related industries 

Trends go beyond products and services, they reflect the evolving desires, behaviors, and priorities of people. Whether it's a global shift, a local vibe, or a niche idea, trends guide us in a fast-paced world. Spot them, act on them, and watch the magic happen.

How to Identify Emerging Trends – Sherlock Holmes Style

Imagine you're stepping into the shoes of a master detective, solving a case that could give you the edge in business, fashion, technology, or any other industry. Instead of dusting for fingerprints, you're analyzing data, tracking social signals, and uncovering real-time insights. Spotting emerging trends is a game of precision; like Holmes' ability to find connections that no one else sees. It's about reading between the lines and making sense of the subtle shifts happening around you. Ready to solve the mystery of what's next? 🕵️

Pay Attention to the Gossip Network

In the world of trends, gossip isn't just about whispers behind closed doors, it's about the pulse of what people are feeling and perceiving about the recent changes. Social media, forums, blogs, and review sites are the modern-day versions of the town square, where opinions and buzz spread faster than ever. These platforms have become the hotspots for conversations that can signal the start of something big. Start by monitoring conversations across various platforms, using social listening tools to track emerging keywords and hashtags. By following the buzz, you'll gain valuable insights into the next big thing before it even has a chance to hit the headlines. Keep your ear to the ground, and you'll always know what people are talking about before everyone else does! 🗣️

It's not just about listening to one conversation and analyzing it in silos, it's about looking for the patterns. The more you tune in to these conversations, the easier it becomes to spot emerging ideas that have the potential to go viral. For example, in the tech world, discussions about a new smartphone feature or a breakthrough in AI can provide clues about the direction the industry is heading. And the best part? These trends often start from the ground up. They are fuelled by real people with real needs, which means they're more likely to resonate with a wide audience and people like you and me.

Keep track of Search Engines – They Know it All

Search engines are the perfect place to start if you want to spot the next big thing. We typically think of them as tools to find quick answers or locate the best restaurants near us 😄 🍔

But in reality, they're constantly tracking the pulse of what people are curious about and searching for. Every search term, from trending DIY tips to the latest fashion must-haves, provides a clue about the growing interests and desires of consumers.

For example, let's say you notice a dramatic increase in searches for "ergonomic furniture for work from home". What was once a niche interest is quickly becoming a widespread priority as more people adapt to hybrid and remote work setups after the pandemic. The surge in the number of searches highlights an increasing trend toward home office furniture, focusing on comfort, productivity, and aesthetics. As a result, companies in the furniture, tech, and interior design industries have started rolling out products tailored to this growing demand, creating a thriving market for remote work solutions.

Keyword Variations

519 Total Volume: **4.3K**

Keywords	Volume	KD %
home office furniture	720	34
chennai furniture home & office furniture store	140	22
custom made home office furniture	90	n/a
home office furniture brands	90	n/a

Questions

4 Total Volume: **30**

Keywords	Volume	KD %
where to buy office furniture for home	20	n/a
where to buy home office furniture	10	n/a
how to arrange office furniture in a home	0	n/a
how to organize home office furniture	0	n/a

Keyword Strategy

Get topics, pillar and subpages **automatically**

- **home office furniture**
  - buy office furniture
  - working table and chair
  - work from home table
  - table for work from home
  - best work from home chair

View all

To harness the power of search engines for trendspotting, use tools like Google Trends, keyword research platforms, and social listening tools to decode these search patterns. Look for recurring spikes in search volume to indicate the growing interest in a specific topic. By analyzing these trends, you can stay one step ahead, ensuring that you're always in tune with what people are most interested in—before the next big wave hits!

Social media – Where Trends Are Born 🚀

In today's digital world, social media is more than just a place to share photos or funny memes. It's the birthplace of trends that can shape entire industries. Platforms like Instagram, TikTok, and Twitter are the pulse of popular culture, offering a real-time snapshot of what's catching people's attention. Whether it's a new dance challenge, a viral meme, or a trending hashtag, social media is where the magic happens. This is where ideas go from zero to viral in the blink of an eye, and spotting these trends early can give you a competitive edge like no other.

By following trending hashtags, viral videos, and key influencers, businesses can spot new trends before they become mainstream. It's not just for engagement, social media is the best tool for tracking the next big thing! ⏭

One such social media trend which has become a way of life for many is becoming a "Minimalist". It's a life philosophy that involves intentionally choosing to have fewer material possessions, commitments, and distractions to create space for what's important. The goal of the minimalist is to live a simpler life with more clarity, time, and calmness. What started as a niche lifestyle trend snowballed into a cultural movement, embraced by everyone from Silicon Valley tech giants to everyday individuals seeking peace and purpose.

Comparing Trends – Welcome to the Trend Olympics! 🏅

Not all trends are created equal. Some trends explode like fireworks, changing industries and shaping cultures, leaving a lasting impact on how we live and work. Others shine brightly for a brief moment, grabbing attention, but quickly fade away into oblivion. In a world where trends can make or break strategies, understanding the differences between them is essential for those looking to capitalize on their potential. Trends can differ greatly in terms of their impact and how long they stay relevant. Understanding a trend's duration and its stage in the lifecycle helps gauge its potential to leave a lasting impact. Here is a summary of some of the most popular types of trends based on their nature and longevity.

Category	Type of Trends	Description
Based on the Nature	Transformational Trends	These trends transform how we live, work, and interact, driving lasting changes in society or industries—like remote work or electric vehicles.
	Incremental Trends	These trends enhance existing ideas with improvements, like seasonal fashion colors or updated smartphone features, without disrupting the norm.
	Novelty Fads	Short-lived trends that grab attention but quickly fade—like the ice bucket challenge.
Based on the Lifecycle	Emerging Trends	Trends just gaining traction, these are the riskiest but can yield the greatest rewards if they stick like AI and ChatGPT.
	Mature Trends	These trends have demonstrated durability and widespread adoption, making them reliable choices for long-term strategies such as e-commerce and renewable energy.
	Declining Trends	Interest is fading away; jumping on trends like traditional print media may leave you chasing a declining wave.

Key Metrics to Track Trend's Potential

When it comes to understanding trends, comparing key metrics is essential to gauge their true potential. ⏱ By examining these factors, we can move beyond surface-level popularity and uncover which trends can reshape industries and societies in meaningful ways. Whether it's the explosive rise of social media platforms or the steady growth of sustainability movements, comparing these metrics helps us make smarter, data-driven decisions about where to invest our time, attention, and resources.

Search Volume

When a trend catches fire, it's not just the experts talking about it, everyone, including your neighbor's dog, will be asking, "What's all the hype?" 🐶

That's a solid indicator that the trend has legs. But don't be fooled by a sudden burst of attention, look for **consistent growth** over time. A short-lived spike might be a passing fad but sustained, long-term growth signals a trend with real staying power. 📈

Regional Variability

Is the trend sparking excitement in just a small corner of the world, or is it gaining momentum across multiple regions? Trends that stay confined to a single region might be popular, but their potential is limited. The real power lies in trends that are taking the world by storm, with people from diverse cultures and countries jumping on board. The more regions that embrace it, the more likely it is to have global appeal. Think of how K-pop exploded from South Korea to dominate worldwide music charts or how plant-based vegan diets transitioned from niche to mainstream food across continents. 📖

Cross-Industry Adoption

When a trend breaks through the boundaries of a single industry, it's a signal that it has **real potential to grow** 🪴 . Trends that seamlessly migrate from one sector to another often reveal a broader cultural shift or consumer demand that can't be ignored. Take an example of blockchain technology, which was initially linked to cryptocurrencies, and has now made its way into industries like finance, supply chain management, healthcare, and even entertainment. Companies are now harnessing their secure, decentralized framework for a variety of applications, including smart contracts and data protection.

Comparing trends is key to making smart and informed decisions. ⚖️ By assessing how trends align with a company's goals, it becomes easier to determine where to invest time, resources, and capital. This approach also helps minimize business risk by highlighting trends that offer significant rewards and those that may not be worth pursuing. Additionally, comparing trends enhances adaptability. By tracking shifts in interest or demand, businesses can swiftly adjust their strategies to stay ahead of the competition. In the current market dynamics, these insights are vital for long-term success! 🥇

Trend-Spotting Tools – Your Ultimate Power Tools

Trend-spotting tools are like online scanners that analyze huge amounts of data to find patterns and predict changes in consumer behavior before they become popular.

Tool Name	What It Helps Do
Google Trends	Tracks global and regional trends, compares topics, and identifies seasonality. Great for spotting emerging patterns in real time.
BuzzSumo	Analyzes the most shared and engaging content online, perfect for discovering popular articles, blogs, and viral content.
Pinterest Trends	Highlights trending searches on Pinterest for discovering upcoming consumer interests, especially in fashion, DIY, and lifestyle.
TrendWatching	Tracks emerging consumer trends across multiple industries, offering students insights into what's changing in the market.
Social Listening Tools (Brandwatch, Hootsuite)	Tracks real-time social media conversations, helping students monitor current trends on platforms like Twitter, Instagram, and Facebook.

From social listening platforms to search analytics and AI insights, these tools provide a glimpse into the future, helping you make informed, proactive decisions. Check out these tools that will turn you into a trend ninja:

Conclusion – Ready to Be a Trend Guru?

With these powerful tools at your fingertips, you're ready to embark on this thrilling journey of trend-spotting ✦ . Think of it like having access to a high-tech radar that helps you track shifts, monitor emerging patterns, and keep you aware of what's happening, whether it's global shifts or the crazy regional buzz. Stay sharp, stay curious, and let your tech guide you through the vast digital landscape.

From spotting the next viral sensation to identifying seasonal shifts, mastering the art of trend-spotting is your newly acquired superpower. Don't just ride the wave—be the one who creates it.

Happy trend-hunting, future trendsetter! 📈 🕵️

Shifting Gears – From Learning to Doing

In the previous chapters, we've explored essential topics such as the skills every market research analyst needs, how to build a powerful online presence, and the art of identifying business trends. But here's the million-dollar question *"Can you simply acquire all of this just by reading this book? The simple answer is "No"*

Achieving expertise in market research, building a compelling online presence, or recognizing emerging trends isn't a single milestone—it's an ongoing process of learning and refinement. Think of it like learning to ride a bicycle . You could read every book about cycling, but until you hop on and start pedalling, it won't happen. The same applies here. The only way to truly master these skills is through consistent, hands-on practice.

So, what comes next? In the upcoming chapters, we'll take all the concepts we've explored so far and put them into action.

We'll focus on applying these concepts step by step so that you can transform knowledge into real change. We'll start by exploring the importance of starting early and why being proactive can give you an upper hand in the current business environment. The earlier you begin, the more time you have to refine your skills, build your network, and stay ahead of the curve. We'll also explore strategies to effectively prepare for the challenges you might face and offer practical solutions to ensure you're well-equipped to handle them.

In addition, I'll offer practical recommendations to increase your chances of landing a job that aligns with your skills and aspirations. It's not just about applying for positions; it's about strategically positioning yourself to be noticed and selected.

Finally, to make your journey easier, I'll provide you with a starter's toolkit; packed with key resources, strategies, and practical steps that will enable you to hit the ground running and approach your preparation with confidence. This toolkit will give you a strong foundation to build upon and guide you toward reaching your goals. The key is to take action now, so you can start making advances in your career.

Let's roll up our sleeves and get to work! 🛠️ 💻

Start Early and Learn Through Mistakes

You've likely heard the saying, *"The best time to plant a tree was 20 years ago; the second-best time is now."* This timeless wisdom serves as a powerful reminder that preparation is everything; especially when it comes to shaping your career and personal growth. Just like a tree needs time to grow its roots before bearing fruit, your professional network, skills, and opportunities require nurturing long before you actually need them. There's no "easy button" that will instantly land you into the job of your dreams. Sorry for being so direct, but that's the reality.

The path to success is often messy. It's about trying, failing, learning from those failures, and then picking yourself up and trying again. Very few people have gotten where they want to without making mistakes along the way. Most successful people would tell you that failures are the best teachers; they teach you what works and what doesn't. It's not about avoiding challenges but learning to bounce back stronger and smarter every time you face them.

Think about how you felt when you tried something new in school. Maybe you were trying to crack a tough math problem or struggling to finish that group project with a tight timeline.

I'll bet that the first time you tried to study for an exam or organize a group assignment, you had zero idea how would you do, right? But with time, you figured it out. You learned how to *actually* study (without falling asleep every 15 minutes), or how to get everyone in the group to actually do their part.

Today, you must be a pro at it.

And that's exactly how it works with learning a new thing whether it's building an online presence or a new skill. It's all about failing, figuring out what went wrong, and tweaking your approach until you get it right.

Still confused?

Let's break it down: How do you start building your skills, networking, and preparing for your future job?

Easy answer: By getting in there and making mistakes.

Sounds simple, but it's the most effective way.

Trust me on this! I'm so confident I could bet my last slice of pizza on it—well, not literally...Just kidding 😊

But seriously, every mistake is a step closer to getting it right. So go ahead, and mess up a little - it's all part of the game!

Embrace the Trial-and-Error Approach

If I were to ask, "Do you want to nail your first interview?" your obvious response would probably be, "Of course, I do!" Well, let me share some insights: you'll likely need a few practice sessions before you truly ace it, and there's a good chance your first interview won't be flawless, and that's okay—it's all part of the learning curve! ∞

The same holds true for things like writing a standout resume, preparing for aptitude tests, or even developing a new skill.

Mistakes are bound to happen, but they are also valuable opportunities for self-correction and continuous growth.

Think of it like playing a new video game 🎮. At first, you might crash, fail, or get stuck at a tough level. But with every attempt, you start to understand the rules, learn from each failure, and improve your strategy. The more you practice, the more you discover the tricks that help you level up. Eventually, what seemed like a difficult challenge becomes something you can easily sail through in a matter of few days.

The same applies to job preparation and career development 📚, the trial-and-error process is essential. No one masters something overnight, and it's unlikely that you'll nail it on your first try. Your first job interview is like a trial cricket match; it may not showcase your full potential, but the lessons you learn from it help you become a stronger player. It's the lessons you learn from setbacks that truly shape your growth. Each challenge you face helps you adapt, refine your skills, and approach future obstacles with a better strategy. These setbacks often hold the most valuable lessons teaching you what works, what doesn't, and how to keep improving. These experiences ultimately prepare you for the next challenge, making you more resilient, capable, and ready for whatever comes your way.

Another key element of the trial-and-error process is feedback , so don't hesitate to seek it out. After an interview or presentation, ask for constructive advice from those who can offer it. This feedback is invaluable—it helps you identify areas for improvement and refine your approach. Like a coach analyzing your performance, feedback provides a fresh perspective on where you can grow. Don't take it personally; instead, use it as an opportunity to improve.

Focus on improving your weak spots and keep practicing the skills that need work. Success isn't a destination, but a journey full of valuable lessons along the way. Embrace trial and error, and you'll be setting yourself up for success.

Practice Before the Big Day

Remember your first interview, your heart's racing, your thoughts feel scattered, and every pause feels like an eternity. Fast forward after a few rounds of practice, you're calm, collected, and walking through questions like a pro. This transformation is a result of preparation and deliberate practice.

The more you practice, the more you familiarize yourself with the process, anticipate challenges, and fine-tune your responses. Practice is where you learn to thrive under pressure. It's a safe space to make mistakes, learn from them, and grow stronger for the real one. By the time the actual exam or interview rolls around, it feels like just another rehearsal, except this time, you're hitting a sixer!

Engaging in mock interviews or practicing with friends and mentors brings a whole new dimension to your preparation. Feedback in these moments is invaluable. You may think you're giving the perfect answer, but someone with experience might spot an area for improvement that you hadn't considered. This type of constructive criticism can be a huge asset. It helps you identify blind spots, correct missteps, and fine-tune your approach. The small adjustments you make after each round of practice can turn you into a much stronger contender. When the big day arrives, you won't just show up, you'll take charge and shine. ☀

Tackling the Placement Challenge: An Eagle's Mindset

Let me stir up some nostalgia and take you back to the placement drive happening at a campus 🏫. The classrooms are bustling with energy, the air thick with anxiety and optimism. Students are glued to their laptops entering final keystrokes perfecting their resumes, carefully drafting cover letters, and rehearsing their interview answers one last time. Everyone's on edge, hoping to impress the recruiters who will soon step through the door.

The long-anticipated guests, the recruiters, make their grand entrance, exuding confidence in sharp suits, warm smiles, and discerning eyes. They're not just there to hand out offers; they're on a mission to sift through the crowd and choose *the one* - pearl in the sea of candidates.

😊 *Kaha hai woh Heera?? ...*

And here's where the story takes a twist;

Students, equipped with their carefully curated resumes,

gleaming GPAs, and answers rehearsed to perfection, march into placement interviews with confidence. They think, *"I've ticked all the boxes—aced every exam, delivered every project, and participated in just enough extracurriculars to stand out. This job is practically mine!"*

But here's where reality does a sharp detour.

The recruiters? They're scanning for something far more dynamic than grades or how neatly you can summarize your academic journey. They're hunting for qualities that make a true professional: adaptability, creativity, teamwork, and real-world problem-solving.

Imagine this: a recruiter leans forward, glances at your resume, and says, *"Your achievements are impressive, but tell me about a time you worked with a team to solve a problem under pressure."* Suddenly, your perfect 10 in thermodynamics feels a little less relevant, doesn't it? The ability to adapt and find a creative solution when things go southwards is what sets you apart from the crowd. Recruiters want to know that you can handle the unpredictability of the real world, not just ace a controlled and hypothetical textbook scenario.

The stellar grades and polished resumes certainly help you get to the interview, but they're not your golden pass to the job. In today's evolving workplaces, it's not about what you know, but how do you apply what you know? Can you think on your feet when a project takes an unexpected turn? Can you bring fresh, out-of-the-box ideas to a brainstorming session? Can you navigate the complexities of working with a diverse team? These are the traits that truly matter.

After all, recruiters aren't just looking for employees, they're looking for future leaders, problem-solvers, and contributors who can drive impact ✦ . Remember, the best answers in an interview often don't come from a script; they come from authentic experiences that showcase your readiness for the real world.

The Employer-Employee Dilemma: Bridging the Skills Gap

On one side, employers are actively searching for the ideal candidate, someone who doesn't need extensive training, can adapt quickly and is ready to contribute immediately. They want someone who will seamlessly fit into the company culture, bring value right away, and make an impact from the moment they're onboarded. Their focus is on efficiency and finding someone who ticks all the boxes on the skill and attitude checklist.

On the other hand, job seekers are equally confident that they're the right fit for the role. They have invested time in building their qualifications, acquiring relevant skills, and fine-tuning their resumes to the prospective role. Job seekers are eager to prove that their abilities align with the job requirements, and demonstrate how they can bring unique value to the company.

At this crossroads, both employers and candidates feel they are in the right position. However, the gap often stems from a lack of relevant, industry-specific skills for the job 📠 . The gap between academic training and the skills demanded by the industry intensifies the skills mismatch. Bridging this gap requires more than just meeting qualifications; it requires technical skills, a strong work ethic, and the ability to communicate effectively.

But as a job seeker, how much effort are you truly investing in acquiring the skills that the industry demands?

Let me share a real-world analogy with you.

You've likely seen a friend or distant cousin intensely preparing for a competitive exam. Now, think about comparing his focused dedication to the efforts of someone searching for a job. This comparison makes sense because both require a strategic approach and a commitment to building a well-rounded skill set. It's not just about knowledge, but about how effectively you can apply that knowledge under pressure. Let's dive deeper into this comparison in the next section.

The Effort-Expectation Equation

When preparing for competitive exams, the relationship between effort and outcome is directly proportional. The more time and energy you put in, the greater your chances of success. A student has to dedicate oneself fully, study for long hours, practice relentlessly, and make significant sacrifices. Social outings, and hobbies, often take a backseat, as every minute is spent honing skills and mastering material. They understand that failure means losing an entire year and having to start over. The stakes are high and the mindset is clear that success comes from consistent efforts and dedication.

On the other hand, job hunting often seems more relaxed and casual . Many job seekers believe that securing a job requires little more than updating their resume, sending out a few applications, and attending a couple of interviews, without putting in much more effort. The sacrifice feels minimal, and the urgency is often lacking. When a job search doesn't pan out, it's easy to shrug it off and think, "I'll just try somewhere else." 💂 The stakes don't feel as pressing, and there's a belief that with a bit of luck or good timing, things will eventually work out.

Here's how the comparison looks:

Aspects	CAT Aspirant	Job Aspirant
Daily Study Hours	*8-10 hours of focused study*	*1-2 hours (if at all)*
Practice Sessions	*Regular mock tests*	*A few interviews, if lucky*
Sacrifices	*Social life, hobbies, sleep*	*Minimal and short-term*
Stakes in Failure	*Complete change of path (a year wasted)*	*"I'll try somewhere else"*

This comparison should be a wake-up call for anyone seriously hunting for a job 💀 . If you're not putting in the kind of effort that leads to growth, skills, and development, then don't expect to stand out. To succeed, you need to treat your job search with the same seriousness as a student preparing for a major exam. This means setting clear goals, staying focused, and dedicating the time and effort required to truly excel in your field. Success doesn't happen overnight, it's the result of consistent hard work. Use this moment to self-reflect. Ask yourself: Are you putting in the level of effort your dream job requires? If you're not, it's time to make a change. Take action today and start making the effort that will lead you to success. 👆

So, Arise, Awake, and Stop not till the goal is reached!

The Eagle's Approach: Think High, Act Sharp

Let's take a moment to reflect on the eagle's hunting strategy, one of nature's most focused and determined creatures. The eagle doesn't fly aimlessly, it knows exactly what it's after. Very high above the clouds, it surveys the landscape with sharp eyes, looking for its prey. Once it identifies its target, it swoops down with laser precision and lightning speed, leaving no room for distraction. This is the kind of focus and dedication that can make all the difference when it comes to achieving your dream job.

Imagine if you approached your job search with the same precision and determination as an eagle hunting its prey, would failure even be an option? Certainly not!

Instead of simply applying to any job that comes your way or sending out your resume without a second thought, you'd set a clear target. Your dream job wouldn't be a vague idea but a well-defined goal you are laser-focused on achieving- just like the eagle. Let me give you a step-by-step approach to how you can do it.

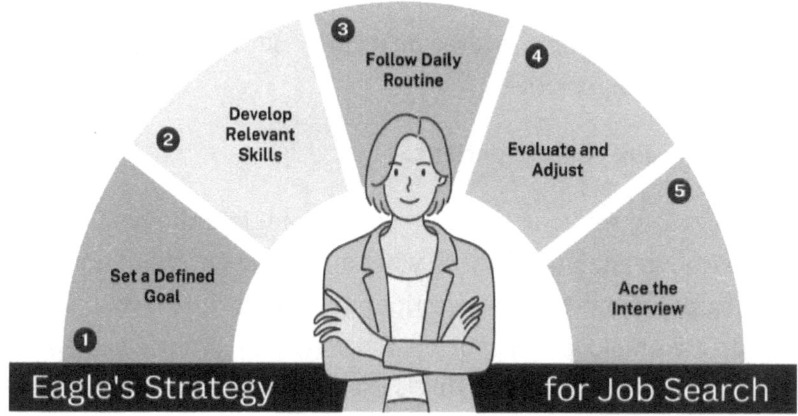

Set a Defined Goal (Your Dream Job)

The very first step in your journey to landing your dream job is defining what that dream job actually looks like. Take the time to really think about your ideal job. Ask yourself questions like *What industry excites me the most? What skills do I want to use every day? What kind of work culture am I drawn to?*

Please write down your dream role, and don't stop here… break it down further by asking yourself more specific questions. *Is it a job at a specific company? A role within a particular team requiring a niche skill?* The more specific you can get, the clearer your path will be. This goal will become your guiding star, a constant reminder of why you're putting in the work each day.

Having a well-defined goal not only gives you clarity but also makes the process of skill-building and job-hunting so much more meaningful. When you know your goal, every effort, skill, and networking conversation is driven by the right intention and purpose. *Without this clarity, even Google can't help you search for what you are looking at* 😕 😕

So, just like the eagle focuses on its prey, set your target, and let it drive your next move.

Develop Skills, Gain Experiences

Once you've set your sights on your dream job, the next crucial step is understanding exactly what it takes to get there. Start by diving deep into the job descriptions of your dream role. *What skills are employers in that field looking for? What experiences are considered essential?* This is the phase where you become a researcher and a strategist for your career.

Take stock of your current abilities by doing your own SWOT analysis—what skills do you already possess that align with the job? If you're great at technical skills but struggle with communication, then you know where to focus your efforts. On the other hand, if you lack a crucial skill entirely, this is your opportunity to build it. ✍️

Take online courses, attend workshops, or find mentors who can help you grow. Whether it's learning a new programming language, improving your public speaking skills, or gaining hands-on experience through internships or freelance projects, make sure you're constantly working on filling those gaps. Remember, the more you learn, the more valuable you become. By proactively understanding what employers expect and working towards building those skills, you're not just preparing for a job, you're preparing for a long-term career. 👨🏻‍💼

Follow a Daily, Focused Routine

Once you've defined your target job and understood the skills you need to land it, it's time to put in the work. This is where your dedication turns into action, and where the real transformation begins. Start by breaking down your larger goal into smaller, actionable steps. If you need to learn a new skill, allocate a certain amount of time each day for focused practice.

Whether it's reading industry-related articles to stay informed or polishing your resume, every action you take should move you closer to that dream job. Just like preparing for a major exam, your efforts must be daily, uninterrupted, and focused. It's easy to get  distracted by social media, friends, or setbacks, but to achieve your goal, you must stay focused and motivated.

Evaluate and Adjust

The journey towards your dream job isn't a straight line, it's a path full of twists and turns. That's why, just like the eagle, you must constantly evaluate and adjust your strategy. The eagle doesn't blindly follow the same flight path if it encounters obstacles or if the winds change; it adapts, shifts its direction, and recalculates. Similarly, you need to assess your progress regularly. The world of job hunting is constantly evolving, and so should you. If your current method isn't bringing the results you want, try something new. Think of it like checking if your GPS is on the right track, or if you're stuck asking cows for directions. 

Maybe you've been focusing heavily on technical skills but haven't had the time to build your networking connections. Or perhaps you've been sending out applications without tailoring your resume to each role. Pause occasionally to reflect on your journey and how much progress you've made.

Evaluate your plans to identify what's working and what isn't.

Ace the Interview

You've worked hard to build your skills, polish your resume, and send out applications. Now, an interview call is your opportunity to demonstrate the knowledge and expertise you've gained and show the company why you're the ideal candidate for the role. This is your time to shine, to show them you're not just another candidate, but *the* candidate they've been waiting for.

Treat this interview as your final exam and approach it with the same intensity as you would for any high-stakes test. Research the company thoroughly to understand its culture, and learn about the role you're applying for. Anticipate questions based on your resume, and rehearse your answers. Focus on delivering your answers in a natural, and engaging way. Dress professionally, as your appearance is the first impression you'll make. And most importantly, be confident. Trust in your abilities and the preparation you've done. Keep your mind calm and your attitude positive. This interview is *your* shot—so make it count! 

Recommendations for Aspirants: The Action Plan

In today's competitive job market, having the right qualifications alone isn't enough. Employers seek candidates who not only have the required skills but can also apply these learnings in the real-world situations. To distinguish yourself, focus on actively connecting with the professional world as you embark on your career journey. 🎬

The first step is developing the skills needed to bridge the gap between your education and your desired career. These foundational skills will help you face the challenges and celebrate the milestones on the way. Here are some key recommendations to guide you through this transition and ensure you're ready to step into the professional world with confidence.

Grab an internship: Your First Corporate Adventure

The academic world has prepared you with a strong technical foundation, but now it's time to step into the dynamic and fast-paced professional world. Internships are the stepping stones that offer you a firsthand look at how the industry operates, providing a

perfect opportunity to bridge the gap between theoretical knowledge and real-world application.

It's during your internship, that you transition from a student mindset to a professional one. Internships help expand professional networks, strengthen resumes, and boost employability. They provide opportunities to explore career interests and refine your long-term goals. Participating in internships equips students with confidence and a competitive advantage in the modern job market.

Pro Tip

Don't wait for the perfect internship. The key is to start—whether it's a small, or big. The lessons you'll gain will be invaluable in the long run. This is not the time to think about a paycheck; you're gaining an experience that will shape your future.

Waiting or Getting Started: A Dreaded Dilemma

One of the most common traps job seekers fall into is waiting for the *perfect* opportunity; that ideal job with a dream salary … in a prestigious company… and … offering unbeatable perks! It's natural to want the best for yourself, but here's a hard truth: waiting for a perfect job often leads to missed opportunities. In a competitive job market, where hundreds may apply for an entry-level role, waiting isn't the best strategy; in fact, it's a disadvantage.

One must understand that career growth starts with progress 🚲 , not perfection. Instead of waiting for an ideal scenario, shift your mindset to action. Apply for jobs that align with your skills, even if they're not your ultimate dream roles. Reach out to professionals on LinkedIn for interviews, attend job fairs to expand your network, and take on freelance or volunteer projects to build experience. Remember that every step, big or small brings you closer to where you want to be.

Pro Tip

Use your current skills and experiences to take the first step. Apply for roles that match your abilities and focus on developing the rest on the job. Growth happens when you're in motion, not while you're waiting.

Stipend vs. Skills: What Matters More?

When you're stepping into the professional world, it's natural to think about the financial reward. After all, a stipend can feel like validation for your hard work. But here's the catch: focusing solely on the paycheck can limit your growth potential in the long run. Think of it as planting seeds for a future that will yield much larger rewards. 💰

While a stipend is nice to have, it shouldn't be your sole motivation. Often, unpaid internships provide incredible opportunities to learn directly from industry experts, attend high-value training sessions, or take on responsibilities that would otherwise be unavailable to entry-level candidates. The hands-on experience and connections you build will serve as a solid foundation for your long-term career growth. These skills will make your resume stand out, and more importantly, build your confidence to navigate your future roles.

Pro Tip

Treat your first internships as investments in your future. Focus on what you're learning, not just what you're earning. If the experience helps build the skills, knowledge, and connections needed for your dream job, it's worth it.

Get Certified: Your Superpower

Certifications are like power-ups in your career journey. They help you differentiate yourself and signal to employers that you're serious about your skills and ready to deliver.

Why are certifications so important? Employers typically seek tangible evidence that you can start contributing right away. A relevant certification signals that you already have the necessary skills to perform the job. It also provides recruiters with an added layer of confidence, making them more likely to  give you a chance. Research what's in demand in your industry and choose programs that are recognized and valued by employers. This strategic approach will ensure that your certification adds real value to your professional growth and enhances your marketability.

Pro Tip

Certifications open doors to valuable networks and resources. Take advantage of these opportunities to connect with peers and industry leaders, enhancing your skills and professional network- a win-win for your career!

Final Thoughts: You're Ready to Go!

Congratulations! You've gathered the skills, insights, and strategies you need to set your career in motion. The world is full of opportunities, and it's waiting for someone with your passion, talent, and drive to seize them. Now, it's time to move beyond dreaming about your future and start actively creating it. Your career isn't a sprint, but it's not a spectator sport either. Sitting on the sidelines and waiting for the "perfect" moment won't get you anywhere. You've learned the importance of taking action, whether it's applying for internships, gaining experience, or earning certifications that open doors. Every small step you take will take you closer to getting a job.

The key now is to maintain momentum. Don't let fear or doubt stand in your way. While the path may come with challenges, remember that they are part of the process. Learn from setbacks, adjust to new situations, and continually refine your approach.

Adopt the eagle's mindset and let it guide and inspire you at every step. 🪜

So, what are you waiting for? Take charge of your career today, build your skills, and keep striving to be the best version of yourself. The world is waiting, and you're ready to shine! Let the adventure begin! 😊

Developing Self-Skills: Your Launchpad to Success

By now, I'm sure you've figured out the main character of this book—it's you, the superhero 🦸 🦸 Yes, that's right.

You hold the key to transforming your life, overcoming obstacles, and creating a lasting impact. You have the power to write your own story or paragraphs... 😄

But if you're still thinking, "*This sounds great, but where do I even begin?*" don't worry, you're not alone. It's perfectly natural to wonder how to take that first step. That's where I come in! ... *Mai Hoon Na* 🙋 😊

Let me provide you with a starter's toolkit, filled with valuable resources to help you lay a solid foundation for success. These tools will equip you with the basics and provide you with the momentum you need to kickstart your journey. With this toolkit in hand, you'll be ready to chase your goals and take that important first step toward the corporate life you've dreamed of.

But remember, it's not the toolkit alone that will make the difference; it's your effort and dedication that will truly bring about the change. So, promise me you'll approach this toolkit with the focus and commitment it deserves. Ready to begin? Let's dive in!

Learn to Speak the Language

When I first started my career in market research, I had a moment that still makes me awkward when I think about it. Let me share it anyway. I was sitting in a meeting room where the team was discussing a client project. They were tossing around fancy terms like "CAGR," "market segmentation," and "SWOT analysis" as if they were just saying "hello" and "goodbye." I had no clue what they meant, but I nodded along, trying my best to look professional. I threw in a few "Mm-hmms" and "Right, right" just to fit in, all while my mind was racing with the thought: *What in the world are these people talking about?*

Not understanding the basics made me feel like a fish out of water . And that was the moment I realized something crucial; if I didn't get a grip on these terms, I'd be stuck forever. So, I made it my mission to learn the language of market research, and trust me, it wasn't easy at first!

That's why I'm including in this handbook a glossary of essential market research terms. I don't want you to go through the same panic-stricken moments I had, trying to decode jargon while silently sweating. Understanding these terms is key to navigating the world of market research with confidence. You'll soon be throwing around phrases like "competitive analysis" and "data triangulation" like you were born with them on your tongue. And when you master these, you won't just sound like a pro, you'll feel like one too.

And let's be honest, that moment when you can drop "PORTER analysis" in conversation and have everyone nod like you just dropped wisdom from the heavens? That'll feel pretty amazing

So, take a deep breath, dive into the glossary, and start using these terms.

Getting Started: Terminologies in Market Research

Market Size: Market size refers to the total revenue or value generated by a specific market or industry within a given period.

Illustration

Imagine a toy market where all the toys sold in a year add up to $1 million, then the size of the Toy Market is $1 million for that year.

Market Share: Market share is the company's contribution to the total market compared to other companies.

Illustration

*If there are three ice cream shops in a town and together, they sell 1,000 ice creams in a year, and your shop sells 400 of those, your market share is 40% (i.e. 400/1000*100)*

Market Research: Market research is the process of gathering and analyzing data about customers, competitors, and the market. It helps businesses understand trends, preferences, and opportunities to make informed decisions.

Syndicated Research: Syndicated Research is when a company collects data and sells it to multiple businesses. For example, a company might gather industry trends, prepare, and sell the report to different companies in that sector.

Custom Research: Custom Research is when a company does the research specifically tailored to a single business's needs. For example, if a brand wants to understand its customer satisfaction, it will commission a custom study just for that.

Qualitative research: It involves exploring people's emotions, opinions, and the reasons behind their decisions through methods like interviews or group discussions.

Illustration

"A bakery asks its loyal customers why they prefer one cake flavor over another during a casual chat."

Quantitative research: Quantitative research is a way of collecting and analyzing information using numbers and data. It focuses on measuring things like how many, how often, or how much, often through surveys, experiments, or statistical tools.

Illustration

The bakery gives a survey to 100 random customers asking how many of them like chocolate cake among other variants and 70 of them say "Yes" to chocolate cake.

SWOT ANALYSIS: SWOT analysis is a way to examine a business's Strengths, Weaknesses, Opportunities, and Threats. It helps businesses understand what they are good at, what needs improvement, what chances they can grab, and what risks they should watch out for.

Illustration – SWOT analysis of the Coffee Shop

Strengths: Delicious coffee and a cozy atmosphere.

Weaknesses: Limited seating space.

Opportunities: Adding a delivery service to reach more customers.

Threats: A new coffee shop opening nearby.

5Ps of Market:

The 5Ps in marketing are Product, Price, Place, Promotion, and People, which are key factors businesses use to sell their products or services successfully.

Illustration – 5 Ps of Marketing

Product: Sells trendy, quality clothes (poor quality clothes won't sell well)

Price: Offers reasonable prices (too expensive, people may avoid).

Place: Available in malls and online (hard-to-find stores lose customers)

Promotion: Uses social media ads and sales (no ads, fewer people notice).

People: Has helpful sales staff (rude service makes customers leave)

Funnel analysis: Funnel analysis is a way to track how customers move through steps, like discovering a product, showing interest, and finally buying it. It helps businesses understand where they lose customers and where they can improve.

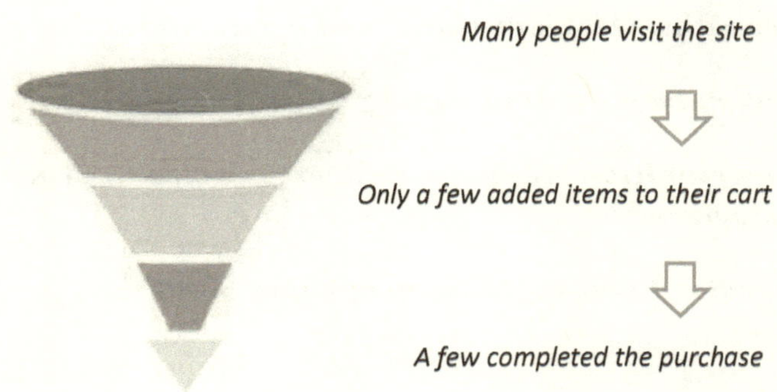

Cohort Analysis: Cohort analysis is a method of studying groups of people who share a common characteristic or experience over time. It helps businesses understand how different groups behave or perform in specific situations, like customer retention.

Illustration

The company tailors marketing strategies for two cohorts: online-acquired customers (Cohort 1) and offline-acquired customers (Cohort 2)

Cluster Analysis: Cluster analysis is a technique used to group similar items or people based on shared characteristics. It helps businesses identify patterns or segments within data, such as grouping customers by their buying habits.

Illustration

"Categorizing customers according to their shopping behaviors, such as those who occasionally buy luxury items versus those who make frequent purchases."

Please note: *Cluster analysis identifies patterns to create groups, while cohort analysis tracks groups defined by time or a shared starting point.*

Net Promoter Score (NPS): Net Promoter Score (NPS) is a metric used to measure customer loyalty by asking how likely customers are to recommend a product or service to others. It helps businesses understand customer satisfaction and predict growth.

Illustration:

"Customers rate the likelihood of recommending the product after purchase: 9-10 are promoters, 7-8 are passive, and below 6 are detractors."

Customer Lifetime Value (CLV): Customer Lifetime Value (CLV) is the total revenue a business expects to generate from a customer, throughout their entire relationship. It helps companies assess a customer's value and determine how much they can invest to retain them.

Illustration:

"A customer pays $10 per month for a subscription and stays for 3 years. So, CLV = $10 x 36 months = $360. The business expects to earn $360 from this customer over their entire relationship."

Key Performance Indicators (KPIs): A KPI is a measurable value that demonstrates how effectively an individual, team, or organization is achieving a business objective.

Illustration:

"A sales team's KPI could be "monthly sales," while a customer service team's KPI might be "average time to respond to customer inquiries."

Porter's analysis: Porter's Analysis, also known as Porter's Five Forces, is a framework used to understand the competitive forces in an industry. It allows them to create strategies that enhance their market position and manage competitive challenges.

Illustration: Porter's analysis of a coffee shop

Threat of New Entrants: A new coffee shop can easily open nearby, increasing competition.

Bargaining Power of Suppliers: Coffee bean suppliers can raise prices, affecting profits.

Bargaining Power of Buyers: Customers may demand discounts or switch to cheaper options.

Threat of Substitutes: People might choose tea, energy drinks, or homemade coffee instead.

Industry Competition: Competing coffee shops offer similar products, creating tough competition."

Competitive Analysis: Competitive analysis involves studying your competitors to identify their strengths, weaknesses, and strategies to gain a market advantage.

Illustration

"A smartphone company might analyze competitors' product features, pricing, and customer satisfaction to develop better devices and marketing strategies."

Market Segmentation: Market segmentation involves dividing a market into smaller groups based on similar characteristics or needs. It helps businesses understand their customers better and tailor products or services to meet specific needs. It improves customer satisfaction, marketing efficiency, and overall profitability.

Illustration

"A shoe brand might segment its market into sports shoes, casual wear, and formal shoes to target different customer needs."

Forecasting: Forecasting is the process of using historical data, current trends, and market insights to predict future outcomes or demand. It helps businesses make informed decisions about inventory, staffing, budgeting, and strategy.

Illustration

"A movie theater forecasts ticket sales for a blockbuster release by analyzing pre-release buzz and past similar movie trends."

Data Triangulation: Data triangulation is a research method where multiple sources, methods, or perspectives are used to cross-check and validate data, ensuring more accurate and reliable results. This approach helps reduce biases that may arise from using a single source or method.

Illustration

"A company studying consumer preferences may use surveys, focus groups, and sales data to better understand customer behavior. By comparing insights from these different methods, the company can verify its findings and make more accurate decisions."

Marketing Collaterals: Marketing collaterals are materials used to promote a product, service, or brand, such as brochures, flyers, or press releases.

Illustration

"A company may create a brochure to showcase its new product features, which is then distributed to potential customers at trade shows or through online channels."

Content Marketing: Content marketing is creating and sharing valuable content to attract and engage a target audience.

Illustration

"A company may create blog posts or videos about industry trends to inform potential customers and enhance brand awareness."

Search Engine Optimization (SEO): Search Engine Optimization (SEO) is the method of enhancing a website to increase its ranking in search engine results, making it more visible to users.

Illustration

"A business can improve its website by using relevant keywords, creating valuable content, and speeding up loading times. SEO includes on-page tactics like optimizing text and images and off-page strategies like getting links from trusted websites to increase traffic and visibility."

Long-tail keywords: Long-tail keywords are longer, more specific search phrases that users type into search engines. These keywords often have lower competition and can attract more targeted visitors.

Illustration

"Instead of using a broad keyword like "laptops," a long-tail keyword would be "best lightweight laptops for students under $500." This specific phrase targets users looking for a particular product, increasing the chances of attracting relevant traffic."

TAM (Total Addressable Market): This is the total demand for a company's product or service in a market, assuming there is no competition. It represents the biggest possible market size.

Serviceable Available Market (SAM): SAM is the part of the TAM that the company can target with its products and services, based on its capabilities and geographical reach.

SOM (Serviceable Obtainable Market): SOM is the portion of the SAM that the company can realistically capture, considering competition, marketing, and sales efforts.

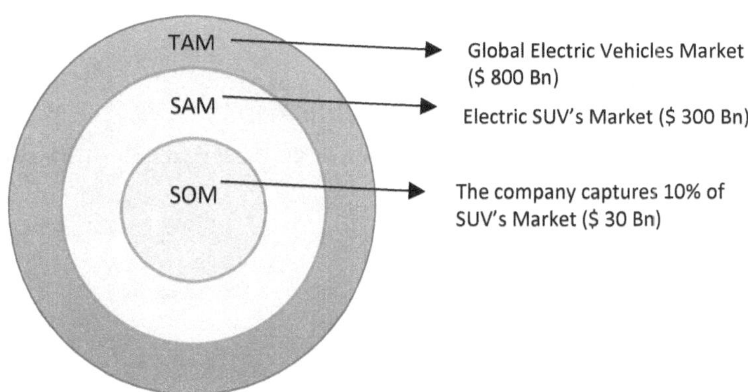

Knowing the industry-specific terminologies is like having the user manual for a high-tech machine, like a sophisticated 3D printer. Just as you wouldn't try to operate a 3D printer without understanding its settings and functions, you can't navigate your industry effectively without mastering its language. These terms act as your guide, unlocking deeper insights and enabling you to make smarter decisions faster.

In essence, knowing these terms:

✔ **Saves time** – You'll spend less time Googling what people are talking about.

✔ **Improves communication** – It allows you to speak confidently and clearly.

✔ **Build credibility** – People will respect your knowledge and expertise.

✔ **Boosts your learning curve** – You'll grasp concepts faster by understanding the context.

So, the next time you hear a new term, don't just let it pass by – dive into it, learn its meaning, and watch how it accelerates your professional growth. 📈

Work Smarter, Not Harder

Let's talk about something we all either fear or try to avoid: data 📊 If you've ever faced a massive pile of numbers, charts, or endless rows in Excel, you've probably found yourself eyeing the nearest exit 🏃 💣

There's that moment when you think, *"Am I actually analyzing data, or am I slowly losing my mind?"* 🦉

But here's the thing: market research is all about data; finding patterns, analyzing them, and discovering insights that can make a real difference. So, yes, it's important, but it can also feel pretty overwhelming at times.

I'll never forget the first time I was handed an Excel spreadsheet full of data to analyze. I just stared at it for a solid five minutes, thinking, "How did I end up here?"

I could almost hear the spreadsheet laughing at me 😵 🤪

But then, like a plot twist in a movie, I stumbled upon something magical.

Excel shortcuts… Oh yes, they exist.

And when I first discovered them, it was like someone handed me a wand and said, *"You're a wizard now, Harry."*

Tasks that used to take me hours suddenly started taking a few minutes. It was a game-changer. With a couple of keystrokes, boom! you're zooming through your data like a seasoned pro. It's like you've been given the secret to turning frustration into success. Suddenly, you're not just getting things done faster, you're getting them done with the kind of confidence that could only be described as "superhuman." Now, imagine what you could do with all the time you save! 😬 😬

Learn the Masterstrokes!

Shortcuts	What it does
Ctrl + F	Displays the Find dialog box.
Ctrl + H	Displays the Replace dialog box.
Ctrl + G	Displays the Go To dialog box.
Ctrl + Page Up	Moves to the previous edit location.
Ctrl + Page Down	Moves to the next edit location.
Ctrl + Z	Undoes the last action.
Ctrl + C	Copies selected text or graphics to the Office Clipboard.
Ctrl + X	Cuts selected text or graphics to the Office Clipboard.
Ctrl + V	Pastes the most recent addition to the Office Clipboard.
Alt + Shift + R	Copies the header or footer used in the previous section of the document.
Ctrl + Alt + V	Shows the Paste Special dialog box.
Ctrl + Shift + V	Pastes the formatting only.
Ctrl+1	Sets single lines pacing.
Ctrl+2	Sets double line spacing.
Ctrl+5	Sets1.5 line spacing.
Ctrl+0 (zero)	Adds or removes one line space preceding a paragraph.
Ctrl + E	Switches a paragraph between centered and left alignment.
Ctrl + J	Switches a paragraph between justified and left alignment.
Ctrl + R	Switches a paragraph between right and left alignment.
Ctrl + L	Applies left alignment

Shortcuts	What it does
Shift + End	Selects to the end of a line.
Shift + Home	Selects to the beginning of a line.
Shift + Down Arrow	Extends the selection one line down.
Shift + Up Arrow	Extends the selection of one line-up.
Ctrl + Shift + Down Arrow	Extends a selection to the end of a paragraph.
Ctrl + Shift + Up Arrow	Extends a selection to the beginning of a paragraph.
Shift + Page Down	Extends a selection one screen down.
Shift + Page Up	Extends a selection one screen up.
Ctrl + Shift + Home	Extends a selection to the beginning of a document.
Ctrl + Shift + End	Extends a selection to the end of a document.
Ctrl + A	Select the entire document.
Ctrl + D	Opens the Font dialog box to change the formatting of characters.
Ctrl + Shift + <	Decreases the font size by one value.
Ctrl + Shift + >	Increases the font size by one value.
Ctrl + [	Decreases the font size by 1 point.
Ctrl +]	Increases the font size by 1 point.
Shift + F3	Changes the case of letters.
Ctrl + Shift + A	Applies or removes All Caps.
Ctrl + B	Applies or removes bold formatting.

Shortcuts	What it does
Ctrl + Equal Sign	Applies or removes subscript formatting.
Ctrl + Shift + Plus Sign	Applies or removes superscript formatting.
Ctrl + Spacebar	Removes character formatting.
Shift + Alt + Page Down	In the top cell, select a column from the top to the bottom.
Shift + Alt + Page Up	In the bottom cell, select a column from the bottom to the top cell.
Alt + Ctrl + Full Stop	Inserts an ellipsis.
Tab	Select the next cell's contents.
Shift + Tab	Select the preceding cell's contents.
Ctrl + M	Indents a paragraph from the left.
Ctrl + Shift + M	Removes a paragraph indent from the left.
Ctrl + T	Creates a hanging indent.
Ctrl + Shift + T	Reduces a hanging indent.
Ctrl + Q	Removes paragraph formatting.
Ctrl+F9	Inserts a blank field.

Shortcuts	What it does
Shift + Enter	Starts a new line in a paragraph.
Ctrl + Enter	Inserts a page break.
Alt + Ctrl + C	Inserts the copyright symbol©.
Alt + Ctrl + R	Inserts the registered trademark symbol®.
Alt + Ctrl + T	Inserts the trademark symbol™.
Ctrl + N	Starts a new blank document.
Ctrl + O	Displays the Open dialog box.
Ctrl + W	Closes the active document.
Ctrl + S	Save a document.
Ctrl + P	Displays the Print dialog box.
Ctrl + Shift + K	Applies or removes Small Caps.
Ctrl + U	Applies or removes underlining.
Ctrl + Shift + W	It applies to underlined words but not spaces.
Ctrl + Shift + D	Applies or removes the double underline.
Ctrl + Shift + H	Applies or removes hidden text formatting.
Ctrl + I	Applies or removes italic formatting.

Now, I know these shortcuts might seem small and insignificant at first, but trust me when I say they will completely transform your workday. They're like the little hacks that make a huge difference, like adding a tiny bit of salt to your soup 🧂 🧂 . You don't notice it at first, but once it's there, everything tastes better, and you're wondering why you never did it before. The more you use these Excel shortcuts, the more you'll feel like a productivity machine 📠 like you're running on some kind of secret power that no one else knows about.

So, here's the challenge: start using these shortcuts. Get comfortable with them, and watch as your productivity skyrockets 🚀 . Before you know it, you'll be the one helping your team navigate complex data while secretly feeling like a data wizard with all the time you just freed up. Trust me, you'll wonder how you ever lived without them ☺ .

Prepare Like a Pro

Alright, let me share a little secret with you: interviews aren't about luck, they're about preparation. After having interviewed hundreds of candidates over the years, I can tell you now, that the ones who stood out weren't necessarily the most experienced or with the highest IQ. The real stars were the ones who came in prepared. They had done their homework, they knew what they were talking about, and they didn't just wing it.

Let me share with you a recent incident of hiring an analyst. There was this candidate who, during the screening test didn't seem like the strongest contender. His resume wasn't flashy, nor did he have any previous experience in this field. But when it came time for the interview, he was on fire. He had researched the company inside and out, knew the key players, and even understood the impact of the latest trends on our industry. It was clear he hadn't just shown up to "chat" he had prepared like a pro. I remember thinking, *Wow! This person gets it* 💯.

No surprise, he ended up landing the job, and it had less to do with his past experience and more to do with the fact that he showed up ready to conquer the interview.

Now, I'm not saying you need to memorize a 10-page report on the company (although, hey, that wouldn't hurt!). But what I *am* saying is this: "Preparation is the Key". To help you prep like a pro, I've included a list of the top 20 interview questions that market research recruiters love to ask.

These aren't just random questions pulled out of thin air—These are the questions hiring managers will likely ask, or at least something very similar. Think of this as your cheat sheet to ace your next interview.

By the way, I haven't included HR questions here... but feel free to prepare to talk about your hobbies... *like mastering the art of balancing assignments with Netflix* and your salary expectations *like enough to fund your caffeine addiction)!*

Top 20 FAQs in Market Research Interviews

1. How would you define a target market, and why is it important in market research?

2. What methods would you use to estimate the size of a market?

3. Can you explain the difference between primary and secondary research?

4. Can you explain the concept of "blue ocean strategy" in market research?

5. What tools or frameworks would you use to evaluate a company's position in the market?

6. How would you assess the impact of pricing strategies on market performance?

7. Explain how you would prioritize which market to enter for a new product launch.

8. How would you determine the effectiveness of a company's marketing campaign?

9. How do you analyze a company's performance based on its financial statements in an annual report?

10. Explain how market research can impact revenue forecasting.

Think of these as your "mock questions," but don't treat them like practice questions; prepare for them as if your job offer depends on them. Because, well, it kind of does! I'm sure some of you have already picked up on what I'm hinting at 😊

Study them, practice them, and go into that interview with the confidence that you're ready to shine. The effort you put into this preparation will pay off big time.

Top 20 FAQs in Market Research Interviews
11. How would you evaluate the return on investment (ROI) for a marketing campaign?
12. What role does cost analysis play in market research?
13. What tools and software are you proficient in for data analysis (e.g., SPSS, Tableau, Excel)?
14. Explain the difference between a focus group and an online survey.
15. What sampling techniques would you use for a large-scale survey?
16. How do you handle incomplete or missing data in a dataset?
17. How do you incorporate AI or machine learning in market research?
18. How do you evaluate customer sentiment using digital tools?
19. How would you use social media analytics for consumer insights?
20. Can you explain how to create and interpret a heatmap visualization?

Study them, practice them, and go into that interview with the confidence that you're ready to shine. The effort you put into this preparation will pay off big time.

Your Launchpad

Let's get one thing straight: this handbook is your ultimate tool to kickstart your career in the market research industry. It will help you build your skills, boost your confidence, and take full control of your career 😎.

Every great journey begins with small steps, and the market research field is no exception. You've got to start from the ground up, and while it may seem overwhelming at first, the effort you put in today will pay off tomorrow. Focus on mastering the basics—get familiar with key terms and the tools you'll be using. Believe me, those small wins will add up fast.

Now, don't get hung up on where you start. Success isn't about having it all figured out right away—it's about rolling up your sleeves and diving in. The best part? You're not alone on this journey. I've got you covered with all the resources and tips you need to grow and level up. Just use them, stick with it, and keep moving forward.

The future is waiting, and it's got your name on it. Success doesn't come to those who wait; it comes to those who take action. So, let's get to work and make it happen. Trust in yourself, and watch how far you can go. The sky's the limit, and the world of market research is yours to conquer! 🏆 🏆

Wishing you the best as you embark on this journey! 🤞 ☺

--------------------------------------- 🍀 🍀 🍀 🍀 -------------------------

----

About Metatech Academy

Metatech Academy is a leading market research training institute based in Pune, India. Offering a diverse range of online and offline certified courses, the academy is dedicated to empowering learners with the skills and expertise required to excel in the dynamic field of market research.

The academy strives to close the gap between academic learning and industry-relevant skills by emphasizing practical, hands-on training. Students engage with real-world projects, case studies, and industry simulations, gaining invaluable experience that directly translates into their professional careers. This approach ensures they not only understand the technologies but also effectively address real-world challenges.

Metatech Academy's courses are designed for individuals at all levels, whether they are just starting their journey or looking to enhance their existing skill set. With flexible learning paths and expert instructors from various industries, students can tailor their education to suit their specific career goals. Whether you're a professional looking to reskill, Metatech Academy offers the resources and support to help you succeed.

Beyond certifications and technical expertise, Metatech Academy offers access to a vast alumni network for mentorship and career guidance, along with opportunities for paid and unpaid internships in both remote and offline formats. It also provides strong placement support through its network of industry partners, helping students secure jobs that align with their skills and career aspirations. This comprehensive approach ensures graduates are equipped with both practical experience and valuable professional connections for a successful career in market research.

www.metatechacademy.com

Continuous learning is the fuel that drives innovation, growth, and success. It's not about being the smartest person in the room, but about being curious, adaptable, and committed to staying ahead of the curve.

9 798896 731481